simple

bead & mosaic

+style+

simple

bead & mosaic

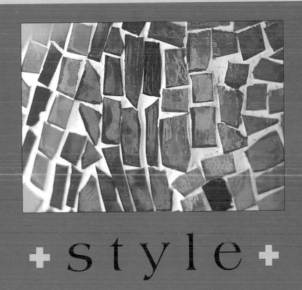

+style+

KARIN HOSSACK

Photographs by Lucinda Symons

Watson-Guptill Publications/New York

Acknowledgments

The author would like to thank Vjera Pandol for her tireless, perfect stitchery on the embroidered cushions and tasseled tablecloth, and to Sue Radcliffe for her unequivocal techniques with plaster and mosaics on the mirror frame, mosaic plate and mosaic background on the bathroom back splash. Thank you both for your spirits of adventure and creativity.

Credits

The publishers would like to thank the following companies for supplying props for the photography of this book. The Blue Door, 15 Church Road, Barnes, London, (0181 748 9785), for the garden chair, page 16; the metal table and the side table, page 35. Purves & Purves, 80-83 Tottenham Court Road, London, (0171 580 8223), for the table, page 21; the chair, page 26; the vase, page 61. Summerhill & Bishop, 100 Portland Road, London, (0171 221 4566), for the chopping board, page 22; the board, wooden plate and bowl, page 25; the china, wooden plate, fork and spoon, pages 26 and 28-29; the linen, page 53; the large bowl, page 65.

Published by MQ Publications Ltd
254-258 Goswell Road, London EC1V 7EB

Copyright © MQ Publications Ltd, 1999

Text © Karin Hossack 1999
Photographs © Lucinda Symons 1999

First published in the United States in 1999
by Watson-Guptill Publications, a division of BPI Communications, Inc.
1515 Broadway, New York, NY 10036
Library of Congress Catalog Card Number: 98-61151
ISBN: 0-8230-4805-5

Printed in Italy

1 2 3 4 5 6 7 8 9 / 06 05 04 03 02 01 00 99

contents

✚

introduction 6

working with beads

working with mosaics

putting it together

In fact, the patterns for many of the projects readily encourage individuality. The butterfly and marigold shapes for the organza curtain can be arranged any way you choose, depending on where you are going to hang the finished curtain. The effect will still be the same. The sheer silk organza with the light tracing of beadery will beckon the sun's rays and warm the light filtering through. There are endless combinations in which bead patterns can be applied in the screen and salad bowl projects. By taking the time to work out a flowing unifying pattern you will find the end result even more satisfying.

The most minimal knowledge of knitting and crocheting is needed to work the knitted hemp curtain or the twine waste paper basket. If you've never tried knitting before, the hemp curtain is an inspired place to start. Casting on, the most difficult step in the whole project, can usually be done for you by a friend or by a helpful expert at a knitting or craft store. The sewing required in some of the other projects has been kept to the minimum of tacking and back stitch, and the knots used to space the beads in the room screen are no more complicated than a standard overhand knot that we use everyday.

Making a project that will live in your home requires some regard for choosing the color scheme and size of the project so that it does not compete with your home style, but blends in gracefully with your existing best-loved objects. Look carefully at your own choice of palette, try to see it with fresh eyes to make your projects harmonize with your furnishings and wall colors. When approaching the projects, give them the time that each one requires for a stunning result to be achieved. Mosaics can take days because you need to give the grout time to dry between stages, while some of the bead items are quick and easy to finish once a pattern has been established.

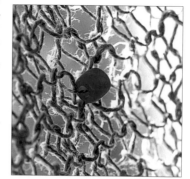

All the objects presented in this book are designed to be able to work in many types of domestic settings whether traditional or contemporary, as the root materials of all the projects spring from a source of nature. The comprehensive step-by-step instructions will guide you through the projects, and by using variations of colors, sizes, and patterns, you will be able to create beautiful crafts with your own signature.

INTRODUCTION

working with beads

Whether you choose to decorate a wire hanging basket with tinkling silver bell beads, add dazzling bead tassels to a vibrant tablecloth, or turn your hand to bookbinding for a photograph album with embossed beadwork, there are endless combinations in which beads can be applied to household objects. The techniques used in these projects will not make any greater demand on your skills than those of sewing, knotting, knitting, and crocheting, all of which are required at fairly basic levels.

Take a humble wooden salad bowl for instance: by encrusting it with colored glass beads in a variety of shapes and sizes, it can quickly be trans-

formed into the center of attention to get back to basics, the wrapped and string demand very little time able materials. Crocheting raffia and runner gives an up-to-date look to garden raffia, allowing our everyday Crocheting also comes into play wooden beads and jute twine in a

The two very different curtains on your table. Or if you really want serving spoons with their buttons and unite two modest but service-bright glass beads into a leafy table crochet and an unexpected use to surroundings to blend with nature. in the waste paper basket using range of warm colors.

in this chapter could both be called

upon to soften the lines of a modern interior or to simply blend into an already gentle decor. You may choose from the refined sheer silk of organza or the rough texture of hand-knit hemp; either one, when backlit by natural light, will allow the beaded patterns to shine through. Maybe you are searching for a way of dividing the space within a room? The beaded screen project presents a flexible means of partitioning a room, inviting light to play, with soft-edged crystal beads strung onto utilitarian garden twine.

And after all this activity, you can collapse peacefully onto your sofa relaxing into a pile of soft bead-embroidered cushions.

WORKING WITH BEADS

organza
curtain

✚

It is always pleasurable to be in a room with sunlight streaming in, but try hanging a pure silk organza curtain in a sunny window and feel the softening, calming effect that envelopes the same room. This curtain is made to simply sheath the window, to wrap the light in a soft sheen, and to project a flash of color from its tiny glittering beads, drawing attention to its ancient Mexican design of floating butterflies and humble marigolds. Everyone from children to adults will be drawn to the intricacy of the beading and charmed by the images. Whether you keep the beadwork as a border design, or as an all over pattern, this delicate window decoration is well worth the time spent to make a project that appears so simple yet can so dramatically change its surroundings.

The outline of the butterfly is made up of lines of tiny beads sewn with a simple backstitch.

bead-embroidered cushion

✚

Enhancing a couch or chair with new cushions is an easy way to bring a fresh look to any living space. By choosing natural fabrics, such as a raw silk dressmakers cloth, and blending in shades of embroidery thread and beads to match this modern palette of hues, an old cushion can be given a new cover to complement new furnishings or decorations, or to add a little sparkle to the existing decor. Make up several cushions in graded sizes and cast them about or pile them up to liven up a bench or couch.

▶ 17

Make up your own delicate designs for a group of cushions or use the same pattern in different colors, mixing and matching the embroidery threads, beads, and fabric.

A pattern of running stitch with colored seed beads threaded on to complement the overall design is so simple, and gives the cushion an air of casual elegance.

waste paper basket

+

It doesn't take much to become accomplished at crocheting, with a little patience. My grandmother tried to teach me to crochet when I was a child. I distinctly remember my first lesson, because she was so frustrated at the twisted mess of string and hook I presented her with, that she bit my hand! Years later I took up a book on crochet and worked through the steps at my own pace.

By incorporating alternating colors of large wooden beads into a striped pattern of red, orange, and natural twines using double crochet, this waste paper basket has a homespun quality that could easily blend into many interiors.

The beads are threaded onto the colored twine and added in as the basket is crocheted.

salad
bowl

✚

Salads are usually thought of as being simple fare, and for special meals we all try to add a few unusual ingredients to make them a bit more interesting. We arrange nasturtium flowers on top and throw in exotic fruits, nuts, and vegetables. By placing this salad bowl on the table, however, everyone will be so enthralled with the decorative beadwork that they will barely notice the contents, and you will be able to give your creative thinking a rest. So this is really a case of a simple design idea making a meal's preparation simple as well! Search out as many different beads as you can find, matching the colors to complement your dinner service, and with a hammer and some nails your next salad will be transformed.

The beads are arranged in an attractive repeat pattern and their positions are marked on the outside of the bowl, before being hammered into place.

serving spoons

+

I love this project for its refreshing use of materials that can be found in any home. Many of us hoard buttons of all shapes and sizes – just in case – but very rarely use them. Most of us would enjoy a chance to show them off for their own attractive qualities. If you need a last minute solution to dressing up a dinner table, this is a quick and easy answer. Find your secret stash of buttons, and mix or match them. Then thread them onto decorative twine and wrap them onto the plainest wooden spoons in the house. Once completed, the spoons should always be hand washed.

The twine is wrapped tightly around the handle to completely conceal the wood and hold the beads firmly in place.

table runner

✚

This handcrafted table runner will give an everyday table an interesting focal point. The repeat pattern of crocheted raffia leaves, embellished with bright glass beads looks at ease both indoors and out. Try other colors of dyed raffia from your local craft store for a different seasonal look.

Since raffia is a natural material, it is not hard on the hands when it is worked into the leaf shapes. It bends and flows as easily as any cotton or wool, and holds its shape beautifully. You can wash it and iron it just as you would any other natural cloth, giving you the confidence to leave it on the table during the most boisterous family meals.

The pony beads create flashes of color along the stem of each leaf and contrast well with the natural tone of the raffia.

hanging
flower basket

+

When a hanging basket is brimming with a careless array of glorious flowers in the spring and summer, it is always easy to step back and admire its beauty. But come the autumn and winter months, the flowers die back, we clear out the moss, and are left with a sad skeleton of bare wires.

By making this wire basket with lots of points and dangling clusters of metal beads, it becomes an object of beauty in its own right, that looks just as attractive when left empty. If you already have a galvanized steel wire basket, you could easily take the framework and embellish it with wire edging and beads, changing the look from a plain utilitarian object to an objet d'art.

The pieces of wire are joined together with simple loops turned at the ends with needle-nose pliers.

Bell cluster beads threaded on to the galvanized wire add a pretty, eye-catching feature to the hanging basket.

tasseled
tablecloth

✚

This festive tablecloth would look good on any table, indoors or out. The colors and stripes in the fabric bring to mind exotic spicy foods, barbecues and brightly colored cocktails. The vivid arrangements of plastic beads catch the light, and also serve to weigh the cloth down, keeping any windy weather in check. If the idea of sewing the points on this cloth is too daunting a task, try making it out of a soft vinyl treated fabric leaving you to simply cut out the points and decorate them with the tassels in the same manner as shown in the instructions.

A wonderful arrangement of small beads in different shapes has been used to make up the colorful tassels.

knitted
hemp curtain

✚

I grew up on the New England coast where, thinking back on it, I can remember most of the shops and restaurants in town had either their ceilings or walls swagged with old twine fishing nets. Some even had old handblown glass floats caught up in the nets that came in a range of purples, greens, and blues.

This knit curtain is my updated version of these old twine nets. My choice of colored beads mimics the hues of the glass floats, but now they have become frosted plastic beads that sparkle when they catch the light. This is a very easy knitting project to attempt. With its repeat pattern of a simple knit stitch, even the most unskilled knitter can approach it with confidence. You do not even purl one stitch.

The beads are added to the hemp curtain in a random color sequence to keep the design free-flowing and interesting.

photograph
album

✚

We all go through periods in our lives when it seems that the celebrations of weddings and births are endless. We spend a lot of time and effort for these special occasions searching out the perfect present. Why not make a personal photo album for someone special and share in their memories in more ways than one. The fiery color with rich gold and copper beads emblazoned on the cover makes this a heraldic gift for newlyweds, and by changing the color for the cover cloth, the idea becomes a baby's photo album. It is just as easy to make two or three of these albums at the same time, leaving some extras for coming occasions, or keeping one aside for your own treasured snapshots. The album can be opened out like a concertina, with the pages laid out flat or flipped over for viewing.

Copper seed beads are sewn in a back stitch over the circle markings to make the Os.

beaded
screen

✚

The beauty of this room screen is that rather than closing off two spaces, it visually divides them, and as the light hits the screen, the soft-edged beads play with the light without glinting. The whitewash effect on the frame gives the screen a soft, natural look that freshens up the natural color of the twine.

Having the frame made up out of hardwood by a woodworker is the best way to ensure that the joints are made properly and the frame won't warp. Once you've got the basic frame, adorning it with beads couldn't be easier. I decided to keep them all crystal clear and I got the largest I could find. If you would like the light to reflect off your beads, then try cut glass beads instead.

A simple overhand knot underneath each bead holds it in place on the twine.

working with mosaics

The art of mosaic is easy to do once you have developed the knack, and the final result of a one-off piece of handiwork will fill you with pride. When approaching any of these projects don't be stingy with the materials, be sure to have the correct amount to finish the job, and be generous too with your choice of colors. Any good tile shop will carry a range of mosaic tiles and I have recently noticed many arts and crafts stores stocking glass mosaic tiles on their shelves.

One way of approaching mosaic is by imitating traditional mosaics such as the fragmented Roman examples we have all encountered in museums.

I have explored this technique in there is a wealth of other materials duce mosaics. The chalkboard, for some rugged pebbles, pressed into can be easily bought in a hardware it and get stuck in up to your elbows embellished with bits of mirror and And there are projects for the nity for recycling old glassware in

the trout encrusted back splash. But and adhesives you can use to pro- instance, makes excellent use of cobalt-blue grouting. Plaster of Paris or craft store. Why not buy a bag of for the mirror frame, which is further colored glass. outdoors as well. A good opportu- the house is with the enlarged street

numbers for the front door, or the stained glass flower vase, which can also stand in for a pretty candleholder with a broad based candle lit inside. The window box will show off any garden flowers or greenery, and the Secessionist style birdhouse will more than likely raise the pitch of any sunrise bird song.

If you want to build up your confidence first, the simple round platter with concentric circles, combining basic techniques and materials of broken and cut tiles is a good place to start. As the desire to move onto something bigger grows, you'll find the plant stand project with its striking lines and colors is ideal.

WORKING WITH MOSAICS

stained
glass vase

✚

This stained glass flower vase is a piece of artwork in itself, but put in a few nodding hydrangea and the design steps back to give the flowers center stage. The fluid pattern of deep blue lines joined together by shades of green and softer sky blues flow around the container in a tranquil design that is easy on the eye even within its embodiment of fragmented glass. The challenge in making this vase is in keeping the pattern subtle so as not to overpower the natural beauty of the flowers, yet interesting enough to never become tiresome as an object in its own right.

Small angular pieces of glass are pressed together over the surface of the vase to produce the flowing lines.

pebble
chalkboard

✚

A chalkboard or a memo board is a necessary object in any busy household. Whether you use it to remind everyone of important times or dates, shopping lists, or chores, it gives everyone the chance to have their say. It is an easy project to make that will happily accommodate any member of the family's findings from the beach or the woods. My pebbles have come from two different vacations: one several years ago on a beach in Cornwall, England, where my two-year-old son stood at the water's edge in his rubber boots throwing stones into the sea while I collected buckets of shingle; and four years later in Wales with a now six year old fighting for the best stones on the beach for his own collection.

A pleasing symmetrical pattern of flower shapes also creates the illusion of zigzags and lines up and down the side panels of the chalkboard.

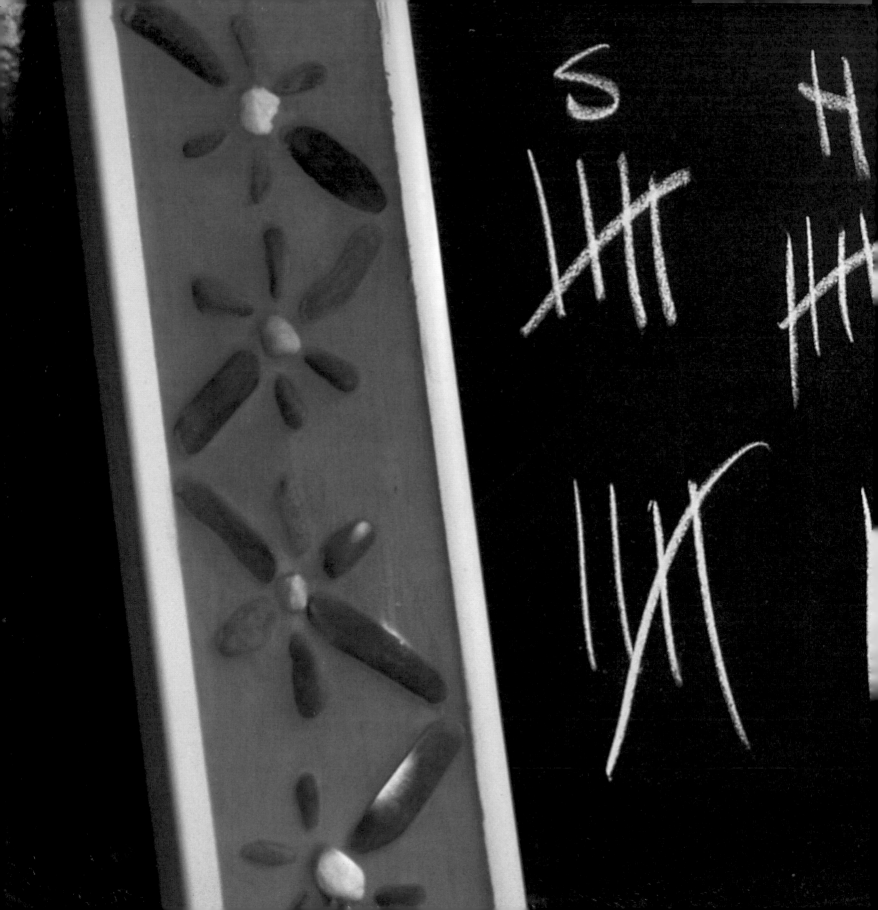

round
platter

✚

This platter for me conjures up images of summer-time, with strawberry shortcake, lemonade, and watermelon piled high on picnic tables with the sun shining and bumblebees buzzing all around. Yes, this plate is definitely for taking out laden with fruits to warm gently in the sun. Enjoy it for its simplicity of design – the stark definition of color and the contrasting elements of broken white tiles against rows of perfect red squares. Try making it up in your own choice of colors to match your summer tableware or use it as a centerpiece in red and white, and experience for yourself the magic of summer.

The shards of white tile are shaped with tile nippers so that they fit neatly into the circle pattern.

house
numbers

✚

With numbers this size, your friends will always be able to find you! I think that they would look perfect on a shingled house by the beach (where a good alternative would be to inset beach glass), or attached to a stone wall at the bottom of a drive. The copper surround used to hold the cement will, with time and the elements, turn a soft verdigris that will blend in with most backgrounds like moss on a stone path. Depending on how many numbers you need, you may want to adjust the size accordingly, but keep them big and bold and let the world know where you are.

The body of the number is made up of white cement with scraps of colored glass pushed into the mixture as it sets.

w i n d o w
b o x

✚

Use a simple mosaic design to give an ordinary window box or flower pot a little zest. This project will always look good, even if it is only filled with greenery. I am drawn to this fig leaf pattern with its soft, rounded edges, echoing the petals of a flower but not trying to grab attention. There's plenty of scope for flowers to show themselves off, and a pleasing balance can easily be met between pot and foliage when you keep the planting soft and simple. A window box does not always have to be placed on a window sill. It can be moved around the garden from path to table, grouped with other plant pots, or left standing alone to make a special statement.

The mosaic is made up of small squares of colored tiles that are shaped with tile nippers to fit the curves of the fig leaves.

mirror
frame

✛

Plaster of Paris is a wonderful natural material to work with. In each of its three states it becomes a different body. As a dry powder it is heavy and brilliantly white. Mixed with water it becomes warm and slippery. It begins to hold a shape, but blink and the shape has gone. As you pour it into a mold the consistency changes from heavy cream to Camembert cheese. And once the plaster has set then there's no end to what you can do to transform its shape – drill holes in it, carve it, sand it, or embellish it with mirrors and mosaic tiles. Making this mirror frame will allow you to experience plaster of Paris from its slippery warmth to the smooth satiny finish of a well-polished surface. Build it up with packaging string and top it off with shining jewels!

Fragments of glass and mirror are glued down onto the frame in the hollows around the molded shapes.

SIMPLE BEAD & MOSAIC STYLE

plant
stand

✚

This plant stand with its striking geometric pattern takes its influence from pre-Columbian pottery designs, incorporating a simple, bold pattern that uses three shades of blue with a fiery orange/pink contrast tile. A vase of bright blue delphiniums would look at home on this stand, as would any tender species in a terra-cotta pot brought in from the garden for the winter. But don't hide this plant stand away in a corner with a fading geranium: bring it into the room. Let its slender height and dashing colors make a statement about itself and your living space, while displaying your favorite plant.

Squares and rectangles of different sizes and colors are fitted together to produce the dramatic zigzag pattern.

bathroom
back splash

✛

A lively scene of freshwater trout will quickly become the main focus for any sink in the house. These smiling fish with their mouths agape are lined up just waiting for a splash of water to make them glisten and draw an admiring glance their way. The softest palette is used here, enhanced by the careful choice of ceramic mosaic tiles. These don't actually come in flamboyant colors; they are only available in natural earthy tones which are perfectly sympathetic to the theme of this back splash. You could make this repeat pattern as large as you like, and you'll be surprised at the ease with which you will find yourself creating fish after fish.

▶ 63

The fish shapes are completed first before a watery background, tiled in subtle shades of blue, is filled in.

birdhouse

+

Bring some excitement into your yard. There's not much we can do to support the needs of a bird in its nest. A bird knows far better than we do about how to make the perfect weaving of twigs and grasses. But there's no harm in recommending a few new ideas. A bird nesting in your yard may never have been to Vienna: your bird may not know anything about Hundertwasser or secessionists! Why not take the opportunity to introduce your feathered friend to the simplicity of this bold graphic design with its ornate golden inlays. Get all the birds talking about the amazing tiled building that has been erected in the neighborhood, just the right size for a bird to nest in.

▶ 67

The bold-colored tiles for the birdhouse provide a strong contrast to the black grout.

putting it together

▶ 69

fter a project has been conceived the next step is seeking out the materials from which it will be made. This can often be the most thrilling part, and also occasionally the most frustrating. None of the materials in this book are what I would call "specialized." They are all fairly common products that are easily found in hardware or home improvement stores, craft stores, and garden centers. The tricky part lies in choosing the beads and mosaic tiles that you want to work with. Try to stick with natural materials, and soft earth tones that complement your personal home style.

A good way to approach a mosaic pattern is by cutting up identical size

bits of colored paper and working down to a drawing of what your gives you an opportunity to see together, nipping, cutting, and shap- about mosaic work is that the eye is where you might see some gaping make up the difference and fill in the

out the pattern by sticking these final image should look like. This the variations of fitting the tiles ing as necessary. The great thing very good at filling in the gaps, and surface of grout, other people will unobtrusive space.

Remember when working on and eyes at all times from sharp

craft projects to protect your hands objects and flying shards of tile.

Place tiles and glass in a strong sack and take this outside before smashing them with a hammer and always wear goggles. Wear gloves when cutting tiles and wire. My favorite type are ordinary rubber gloves because they protect my hands from the repeated gripping and cutting motion of the cutters, but they don't desensitize my sense of touch as much as some other gloves can do. Wherever possible, work in an open well-ventilated space when using powerful glues.

Above all, try to have fun when making your projects, and give them the time and care that they sometimes need to fully develop.

PUTTING IT TOGETHER

organza curtain

✚

The colors of the butterflies and marigolds drifting across this organza sheath can quite easily be changed to match your decor.

MATERIALS
◆ *68 x 44in/173 x 112cm white organza (or to fit window with added seam allowance)*
◆ *Twelve café curtain clips, or as many as you need*
◆ *Café curtain tension rod cut to fit the width of the window*
◆ *2oz/50g of size 060 (6/0) seed beads in each color of red, pink, pale green, dark green, pale blue, dark blue, yellow, purple, black*
◆ *Sewing machine*
◆ *Sewing kit*
◆ *White thread*
◆ *Soft lead pencil*

1 Measure the inside dimensions of your window frame, add a seam allowance and cut a piece of organza to fit.

2 Photocopy as many flower and butterfly templates as you want for your curtain.

3 Lay the organza right side up and slide the templates underneath in a pattern of your choice.

4 Trace lightly over the templates with the pencil, then remove the photocopies.

5 Begin sewing beads over the lines with a back stitch, completing each shape from the center out.

6 Sew the beads in place on all the flowers and marigolds, following the color key on the templates. Keep all threads and knots to the back, neat and tight.

7 Hem three sides with a ½in/1cm doubled-over hem pressed in place and sewn with a single row. Make the hem at the top of the curtain ⅝in/1.5cm to allow some leeway for clips.

8 Attach the clips along the top of the curtain. Keep an even spacing in between. Slip the clips onto the tension rod and insert into the window recess.

bead-embroidered cushion

✚

Keep your choice of fabrics natural, with a slightly rough weave to enjoy the contrast of fine, simple embroidery stitches and glittering beads

MATERIALS
- *12in/30cm square machine washable cushion*
- *½yd x 45in/500 x 114cm raw silk*
- *Four 8yd/8m skeins embroidery thread*
- *2oz/50g size 060 (6/0) colored seed beads*
- *Pencil*
- *Embroidery needles and sewing kit*
- *Tracing paper*
- *Tracing wheel*
- *Dressmaker's scissors*
- *Dressmaker's tracing carbon paper*

1 Add a border of 3½in/9cm to the size of your cushion and cut two pieces of silk to this measurement.

2 Photocopy the border pattern to the correct size and trace it onto tracing paper.

3 Place on top of the dressmaker's carbon paper and pin in place to one side of one piece of fabric, leaving a seam allowance of ½in/1cm. Transfer the pattern to the fabric using a tracing wheel. Mark the pattern around all four sides of fabric.

4 Lay the fabric on a flat surface. Split a workable length of embroidery thread into three strands. Thread an embroidery needle (the correct size to get the beads over), double the thread over and knot the end.

5 Embroider the pattern in an even running stitch threading on beads where indicated in the pattern (*see picture next column*).

6 Take both pieces of fabric and place right sides together. Sew a seam ½in/1cm from the edge around three sides. Turn the cover right side out and press in the fourth hem. Iron all edges.

7 Measure and mark with pins 3in/7.5 cm in from the edge of three sewn sides to hold both sides of the fabric in place. Sew around this inner border. Slip the cushion in and sew up the fourth side, along the inside and outside edges of the border.

8 Thread the needle with six strand embroidery thread and make two lines of running stitch ¼in/5mm apart, over the top of the stitching on the inside of the border and around the outer edge.

waste paper basket

✚

This project uses a basic crochet stitch, but make sure you read and understand the instructions before proceeding.

MATERIALS

- *One 1lb/500g ball natural garden twine*
- *One 5oz/150g ball dyed jute twine in each color of red, dark orange, and light orange*
- *Large-eyed sewing needle*
- *Size J/6mm crochet hook*
- *Eighty-four ¹⁄₂in/18mm diameter wooden beads: natural, pink, orange, red*

Finished height: 10in/25cm

1 Using the natural twine chain five stitches; join together with a slip stitch. Double crochet twice into every stitch, place a colored string for a marker at the join. Work double crochet stitch once into every stitch; from then on every other row is an increase row. Work double crochet throughout. Make the increases by first increasing every other stitch by one stitch, then the next increase row every third

stitch, the next increase row every fourth stitch etc. This will keep the disc shape enlarging evenly and flat.

2 Crochet the base to 9½in/24cm across. Place a marker at the finishing point.

3 Begin the sides by crocheting one double crochet into every stitch along the edge. Turn the work so that the crochet hook faces you and work in the opposite direction to which the base is worked. Make five rows in double crochet and cut off leaving a tail.

4 Take the ball of red twine and string 12 beads in two alternating colors onto the

twine. Attach to the tail of the natural twine and continue the sides using double crochet following the pattern below:
3 rows red – bead the middle row
1 row light orange
1 row natural
1 row dark orange – bead row
1 row natural
1 row light orange
3 rows red – bead the middle row
3 rows natural
For the beaded rows, work a bead into every sixth stitch by drawing up one bead and making a stitch behind it.

5 Repeat the pattern. Finish off the top edge by crocheting a slip stitch around the rim. Cut off and work in the end.

salad bowl

✦

One trip to a good bead shop should be enough to gather a superb selection of beads for this project.

MATERIALS

◆ *Wooden salad bowl 6in/15cm tall, 9in/23cm across the top, with walls ¾in/2cm thick*
◆ *Variety of ½in/1cm long panel pins or wood nails to fit the holes in the beads*
◆ *Hammer*
◆ *Dressmaker's measuring tape*
◆ *Soft lead pencil*
◆ *17 crystal disc beads 18mm*
◆ *Variety of colors and shaped beads:*
26 blue pyramid glass beads 6mm
13 orange triangle glass beads 8mm
26 blue round glass beads 6mm
52 orange round glass beads 6mm
13 crystal round glass beads 6mm
26 crystal faceted glass beads 5mm

1 Using a combination of beads of your own choice, lay out the glass beads in a repeat pattern of 8in/20cm wide to get a good idea of how they will look on the bowl (see picture next column).

2 Choose one bead at the top edge of the pattern and measure the repeat distance between each of the same type.

3 Measure around the top rim of the bowl where that bead will be placed and adjust the distance of the beads if necessary to make the pattern fit evenly around the circumference of the bowl. Remember the bowl tapers, so the space between the beads at the bottom of the pattern will be closer than at the top.

4 Mark the positions of the first bead in the pattern using the dressmaker's tape and soft lead pencil.

5 Take the total number of first beads in the pattern and nail each one into place on the bowl using the pins or nails.

6 Following the bead pattern laid out before you as a guide and working one type of colored bead at a time all the way around the bowl, nail the remaining beads into place.

7 Turn the bowl over and nail four large disc-shaped beads onto the bottom, close to the edge and evenly spaced.

serving spoons

✚

Any spoons, twine, beads, and buttons that you find in a drawer or sewing kit would be suitable for this project.

MATERIALS
◆ *Two 8in/20cm wooden spoons*
◆ *Four or five mother-of-pearl buttons in two or three graded sizes*
◆ *PVA glue*
◆ *5yd/6m colored polyester whipping twine, or silk beading cord*
◆ *Large-eyed half round upholstery needle*

1 Arrange the buttons in the sequence you want them to appear on the spoon, thread them onto the twine or cord, working from top to bottom at the tail end of the twine.

2 Leaving a tail of 3in/5cm, glue the twine with a thin line of glue down the center back of the spoon 1in/2cm from the tip of the handle, to where you wish to begin wrapping. Leave to dry.

3 Holding the twine in place at the base of the handle, begin wrapping it tightly around the handle. Push down on it as you go to keep the spacing neat.

4 Wrap approximately 15 times and bring forward the first button. Push it into place on the front center of the handle. Keep the twine tight to hold it in place.

5 Continue wrapping and adding in the buttons with even spacing between each one. Finish wrapping 1in/2cm from the tip of the handle.

6 Tie a small tight knot with the two ends of twine. Thread the needle with one end of twine and draw it through the wrapped twine at the back of the handle and out again 1in/2cm down. Cut off the end and do the same to the other tail end.

7 If the twine or cord that you have used is soft put a small dab of PVA glue on the backside of the knot and glue hidden under the edge of the twine.

table runner

✦

This runner sits happily with a table-cloth underneath, or on its own, leaving the natural color of the raffia to blend beautifully with the wooden surface of the table.

MATERIALS

◆ *Two 3oz/100g skeins natural raffia*
◆ *120 small green glass pony beads*
◆ *14½in/37cm length of ¼in/6mm sisal rope*
◆ *Size H/5mm crochet hook*
◆ *Large-eyed sewing needle*
◆ *Scissors*
◆ *Pencil*

Finished size of each leaf: 7 x 3½in/ 18 x 9cm

1 Take a raffia skein apart and tie the ends together to make one continuous ball. Do the same to the second skein.

2 To make the leaf shapes, using the raffia make three chain, insert the crochet hook into the second chain and double crochet one stitch, turn the work around and double crochet into the first stitch, continue

across in double crochet stitch to make three stitches in a row, turn the work around and double crochet into the first stitch. Work across the row in double crochet to make four stitches, continue turning the work and double crochet into the first stitch to increase the stitch in each row until there are 10 stitches across.

3 Work one more row of 10 stitches, turn the work and begin reducing one stitch from each row by skipping the first stitch in each row and working across in double crochet. The finished leaf shape will have 21 rows.

4 Next work a slip stitch all the way along the edge, slip a knot into the last stitch at the tip of the leaf and cut off leaving a tail of 8in/20cm. Make 12 leaves in total.

5 Set a dry iron to a light heat setting and press each leaf on both sides to flatten.

6 Tidy up all the knots and raffia threads by pulling them through to the underside of each leaf and cutting off the stray ends.

7 Thread the needle with a thin thread-like length of raffia and working from tip to stem stitch the beads in place spacing them every other row apart in a straight line up the middle of each leaf.

8 Thread the needle with a new piece of thread-like raffia and bind one end of the sisal rope by wrapping the raffia tightly from the cut end ½in/1cm up the rope, then stitch through the rope and wind back down, stitch through the rope again and knot in place. Repeat at the other end.

9 Mark the position of each leaf along the rope with a pencil. Sew each leaf in place using the tail of raffia left at the stem end. Keep all knots neat and to the back of the work. Sew the edges of the leaves where they touch with a tacking stitch of raffia.

hanging flower basket

✚

A home improvement or garden store is a good place to find galvanized wire.

MATERIALS
◆ *32 bell cluster beads*
◆ *Six beads shaped like bumblebees*
◆ *One roll fine beading wire 24 gauge/ 0.4mm*
◆ *16oz/500g galvanized wire 12 gauge/2.00mm*
◆ *16oz/500g galvanized wire 14 gauge/1.60mm*
◆ *3in/7cm S hook*
◆ *Round-nose pliers*
◆ *Needle-nose pliers*
◆ *Wire cutters*

1 Cut all the wire lengths for the basket with wire cutters as follows:
Bottom circle: one length 12 gauge/ 2.00mm wire 29in/74cm long
Top circle: one length 12 gauge/2.00mm wire 31in/94cm long
Bottom struts: six lengths 12 gauge/ 2.00mm wire 8½in/21cm long
Decorative edging: 32 lengths 14 gauge/ 1.60mm wire 5in/13cm long
Sides of basket: 24 lengths 12 gauge/ 2.00mm wire 8in/20cm long
Hanging chain: eight lengths 12 gauge/ 2.00mm wire 9in/23cm long
Crown circle: one length 12 gauge/ 2.00mm wire 20in/50cm long

2 To make the top and bottom circles, take each length of wire in turn, close the circle shape by twisting 5in/13cm at each end around each other with the needle-nose pliers. The top ring should measure

9in/24cm in diameter and the bottom ring 7in/18cm.

3 Take the wire for the bottom struts, straighten them out and, using the round-nose pliers, bend the ends into open loops, curving in the same direction. Attach the wires in an even crisscross pattern onto the bottom circle, like the spokes of a wheel, tightly closing all connecting loops.

4 To secure, take a length of fine beading wire and wrap it around the circumference of the circle, enclosing the end of the struts as you wrap.

5 Take the lengths for the decorative edging and with the round-nose pliers, bend each in the middle to form a V. Put a cluster of bell beads on each, bend the ends into open loops, curving towards the back of the shape to make it three-dimensional, rather than flat at the sides.

6 Attach 12 to the bottom circle by securing the loops shut with the needle-nose pliers, placing one V-shape in the gaps between the struts.

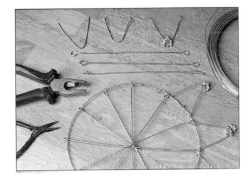

7 Take the wire for the sides of the basket. Leave them in an arched shape and make open-ended loops at both ends, curving

them towards the outside of the arc shape, with the round-nose pliers.

8 Attach to the bottom circle into every space between a V-shape and a strut. Ensure that the arcs curve inwards. Close all bottom loops with the needle-nose pliers.

9 Attach all the top loops to the top circle by crisscrossing every pair of side arcs and then closing the loops with the needle-nose pliers.

10 Attach 12 V-shapes to the top circle inside the crisscrosses of the side arcs. Keep the spacing between the side arcs even. Close all loops securely with the needle-nose pliers.

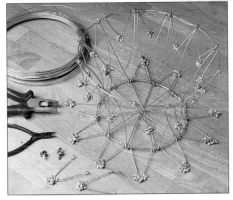

11 Cut six lengths of 4in/10cm beading wire, string on a bumblebee bead and wrap the wire around alternate cross sections of the side arcs. Tighten securely and tie off on the inside of the basket.

12 To make the crown, twist the ends of the wire over each other to form a circle 5in/13cm in diameter. Attach eight V-shaped pieces of decorative edging. Space them evenly and close all loops with needle-nose pliers.

13 Flatten out the lengths of wire for the hanging chain and bend loops into each end using round-nose pliers. Turn all the loops in the same direction.

14 Attach four lengths of "chain" wires to the crown, securing one end of each between every two V-shapes. Attach the remaining four lengths of chain directly into the loops of the four previous ones. Close the loops firmly.

15 Check that the chain wires are hanging properly, four hanging down, and four going up. Attach the four hanging down to the top edge of the basket, spacing them evenly between every four V-shapes and closing all loops.

16 Gather the four top hanging chains onto the S hook and hang the basket in place.

Detail showing a bumblebee bead.

tasseled tablecloth

✚

This tablecloth requires 40 bead tassels. Each tassel has six beaded strands with two beads for a cap.

MATERIALS

◆ 56¾in/144cm square piece of print or striped cotton cloth
◆ 56¾in/144cm square lining fabric in plain or solid color
◆ Sewing thread to match

◆ *Sewing kit*
◆ *Dressmaker's measuring tape*
◆ *One skein contrast embroidery thread for the edge*
◆ *240 plastic "drop" beads (hole across the top), assorted colors*
◆ *1000 one color plastic 6mm round beads*
◆ *240 one color plastic "tube" ½ x ¼in/11 x 4mm beads*

◆ *40 one color plastic "rondelle" ½in/12mm beads*
◆ *40 one color plastic "faceted" ⅓in/8mm beads*
◆ *One roll very fine beading wire*
◆ *Button sewing thread, color to match the beads*
◆ *Round-nose pliers*
◆ *Wire snippers or scissors*
◆ *Dressmaker's pencil or chalk*

1 With the wire snippers, cut 240 pieces of the beading wire 4in/10cm in length to make the tassels.

2 Take one length of wire and attach a "drop" bead to one end. With the round-nose pliers, bend the tail end of the wire and twist it over to stop the bead from falling off. Bead on four round 6mm beads and one tube bead.

3 With the pliers, make a loop at the top of the tube bead (this should be at the center of the wire), and bead the remaining length of wire with one tube bead and four round 6mm beads.

4 Finish with a "drop" bead, twisted securely in place. Use different colors of drop beads for each tassel for contrast.

5 To make up the tablecloth, see the diagram at the back of the book for a cutting guide to the corners. Each side of the cloth has nine points measuring 4¾in/12cm from point to point, with a ½in/1cm hem around the edge of fabric.

6 Use the lining fabric for marking up the measurements with a dressmaker's pencil or chalk. First measure and mark all four corners and then measure and mark nine triangles down each side.

7 Pin or baste the main fabric with the right side out to the lining and cut both together along the marked lines. Keep the two pieces of fabric pinned or basted together until all the sewing is complete.

8 Choose one of the colors in the fabric and cut a workable length of contrast color embroidery thread.

9 Separate the thread into three strands and thread a needle. Sew a running stitch down the sides of each stripe of your chosen color. This will act to hold the two pieces of fabric together.

10 Fold and iron ½in/1cm hems on all the edges of both pieces and using a matching colored thread slip stitch the lining to the main cloth. Iron all edges.

11 Cut another workable length of contrast color embroidery thread and separate it into three strands.

12 Thread a needle with the strands and sew a neat running stitch ¼in/6mm in from the edge of tablecloth (*see picture next column*).

13 Remove all the pins or basting threads and iron if necessary.

14 To attach the tassels to the points, use the button sewing thread in a color to match the beads, knot the end and stitch the thread through one point in the cloth from back to front. Bead on one faceted ½in/8mm bead, then a rondelle bead, then three of the beaded strands by the loops in the middle and draw the "tassel" up to the point.

15 Now bring the needle back up through the rondelle and faceted beads and stitch back through the point in the tablecloth. Pull the beads tight. Make a neat knot at the back of the fabric and cut off. Do this to all the points on the tablecloth.

knitted hemp curtain

✚

This project is even easier than knitting a scarf. Once you've cast on you simply knit and knit and knit!

MATERIALS

◆ *Twelve 3.5oz/100g balls thin hemp twine (available from bead and craft stores)*

◆ *One pair metric size 11/English 0 knitting needles*

◆ *Sewing machine and sewing kit*

◆ *4yd /3.5m of ½in/1cm wide linen binding tape*

◆ *Linen thread to match the color of the tape*

◆ *One thin tension rod or net curtain wire kit 46in/117cm, or to fit window*

◆ *Five hundred ½in/1cm frosted plastic beads in an assortment of colors and shapes*

Finished size 68 x 44in/133 x 112cm

1 Knit a tension sample with some spare twine and adjust the pattern as required to fit your window. Tension: 5 stitches = 2in/5cm; 10 rows = 2in/5cm.

2 Begin unrolling the first ball of twine by pulling the end from the middle of the ball: this stops the twine from twisting. Pull out a workable length and then string on a random selection of 70 beads leaving enough twine to cast on 120 stitches.

3 Cast on, drawing up and catching in a bead in the first stitch, and then every fifth stitch, ending with a bead in the last stitch (*see picture next column*).

4 Begin knitting the curtain. By knitting every row the tension in the twine pulls back on itself keeping the work flat. To create the bead pattern, add the beads in a random color sequence beading every sixth row.

5 Begin the pattern by drawing up a bead and adding it into the knitting on the tenth stitch of the sixth row and then every tenth stitch across that row. Knit five more rows. On the twelfth row begin beading the fifth stitch in the row and then every tenth stitch across the row.

6 Repeat this pattern up the entire length of the curtain beading every sixth row and adding on additional balls of twine.

7 Each time you begin a new ball of twine, draw out a workable length from the middle and string on about 40 beads from a mixed bag.

8 You may need to adjust the distance of the beads and rows according to your tension and the measurements required.

9 When you are about 4in/10cm short of the top of the curtain hang the knitted panel up to let it stretch.

10 Without binding off the top edge of the curtain, pin the tail end of twine to the edge of curtain and leave the rest to hang down.

11 Slip the curtain very carefully onto the tension rod/curtain wire, and place/hook in the window recess. Adjust the height of the curtain by moving the rod up or down in the recess. Leave the curtain hanging in place for at least 48 hours.

12 Readjust the length if necessary by moving the tension rod higher up in the window frame or slip the curtain onto the knitting needle if more knitting is required.

13 Add on or take off as much as is needed to allow your curtain to hang to the required length.

14 To finish the top, slip the loops of the top edge back onto the tension rod and with a large-eyed needle and a length of hemp twine sew in a running stitch across the top through the knit loops on the wire. Make two rows of stitches to keep the knitting secure.

15 Alternatively you could run it through a sewing machine on a long baste stitch, sewing two rows (*see picture next column*).

16 To finish the edges, cut two pieces of linen tape to the length of the curtain leaving enough for hems at the bottom. Hang the curtain up and pin each length of tape along the back edge of the sides.

17 Take the curtain down and sew the tape in place on a sewing machine using a long basting stitch or by hand with a running stitch. Tidy and trim all the ends.

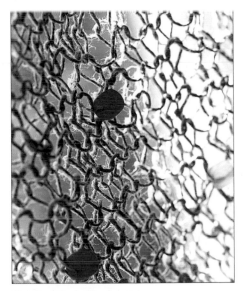

Detail of the knitted curtain.

photograph album

✚

Methyl cellulose has been used as a sizing medium to stiffen the boards and cloth and stop them from warping as you make the album.

MATERIALS

- One (24 x 18in/60 x 45 cm) A3 sheet display board
- ½yd x 50in/500 x 127cm crushed suede
- 12in/30cm square white cotton chintz
- Three sheets artist's rag/handmade paper, 22½ x 8¼in/57 x 21cm
- 2oz/50g copper seed beads
- 2oz/50g gold tube beads
- Colored thread to match beads
- Two sheets decorative endpapers, 11½ x 8⅜in/29 x 21½cm
- Methyl cellulose
- PVA glue
- Soft bristle glue brush
- Pencils and ruler
- Artist's scalpel or craft knife
- Circle stencil

- Beading needle
- Scissors
- Chalk pencil
- Newspaper
- Greaseproof paper
- Heavy books
- Bone folder

1 Cut two cover boards 8⅝ x 11¾in/22 x 30cm from the display board, and two pieces of suede 10¼ x 13¼in/26 x 34cm. From the chintz cut two pieces 8¼ x ⅞in/ 21 x 2.2cm and two pieces 8¼ x ½in/ 21 x 1.2cm.

2 Mix 2oz/50g methyl cellulose with 4fl oz/100ml cold water until smooth. Stir in an equal amount of PVA glue and mix thoroughly. This makes a sizing medium for all the card and cloth.

3 Place the cover boards on newspaper and with the glue brush paint a thin layer of sizing medium over the surface of each. Keep the brushstrokes in the same direction. Leave to dry.

4 Paint a second coat with brushstrokes in the opposite direction and leave to dry. Repeat on the other side of the board.

5 Place the crushed suede face down on clean newspaper and paint with a thin coat of sizing medium. Leave to dry. Do the same with the chintz strips.

6 Fold all the paper sheets in half using a bone folder or the edge of a pencil or ruler to get a flat crisp edge.

7 To make the concertina pages for the album, take one ½in/12mm strip of chintz and paint the sized side with a thin layer of PVA glue. Align the edges of two sheets of paper on the center of the strip (folded hills of the sheets facing up), and press into place.

8 Paint a thin layer of glue on the second piece of chintz and attach the third sheet of folded paper to the second in the same way. Allow to dry flat.

9 Fold the pages carefully along the joins and folds into a neat flat concertina.

10 Place both pieces of crushed suede right side down on a hard surface. Place a cover board in the middle of each, ensure that all edges are even, and trace around the board with the chalk pencil. Put the piece for the back and the cards aside.

11 Working along the chalk lines on the front piece, lightly mark a point with the chalk pencil 1⅛in/3cm in from the corner of each long side. Then mark every 1⅝in/4cm in between the two points. Mark points at similar intervals along both short sides.

12 Using a ruler, line up the dots and mark every 1⅝in/4cm across and down the material with the chalk pencil to give you seven rows across the album and five rows down.

13 In pencil, mark the top left corner dot with an X, then mark every other dot with an X, row by row down the album.

14 Center a circle stencil of ½in/1.2cm diameter over each remaining dot and draw a circle with a sharpened pencil. When you turn the fabric over there should now be a distinct impression of the Os and Xs pattern.

15 Thread a beading needle with thread to match the color of the beads and sew approximately 15 seed beads over each circle outline with a back stitch.

16 Sew four tube beads over the markings for the Xs (see picture next column).

17 Lay both pieces of suede right side down on clean newspaper. Brush a thin coat of PVA glue across the back of one piece, lay a cover board in place inside the chalk lines, turn it over, and with a bone folder or the side of an unsharpened pencil gently smooth out all the air bubbles.

18 Turn it face down again: if the PVA around the edges has begun to dry, touch them up again. Trim the corners of the cloth to ⅜in/1.5cm from the corner of the card. Fold the top and bottom edges onto the board smoothing firmly into place.

19 Before folding in the side edges, tuck the corners in as you would do the corners on a hospital bed. Fold over the sides and smooth and press into place.

20 Repeat with the other cloth cover. Leave to dry.

21 To glue the pages to the covers, brush about ¼in/5mm in along one edge of the ⅞in/2.2cm wide chintz with PVA. With the paper concertina in front of you with the chintz edges to the left and folded edges to the right, glue the edge of the chintz to the top edge of the back page.

22 Take the other strip, brush with PVA in the same way and stick to the back edge of the top page. Leave to dry.

23 Use a bone folder or pencil edge to fold the extra chintz over, paint the back with PVA and attach to the cover boards one at a time. Leave to dry.

24 Adjust the size of the end papers if neccessary and brush with PVA glue.

25 Stick in the center of the boards over the chintz with a ⅛in/4mm border of suede showing. Press out all air bubbles with a bone folder or edge of a pencil.

26 Place a piece of greaseproof paper between the cover board and pages and press the album under a stack of heavy books overnight.

beaded screen

✦

Have a carpenter make the screen up for you to the dimensions below. It is important to use a hardwood so that the frame doesn't warp.

MATERIALS

◆ *2 by 2 oak/4cm thick square oak*
◆ *Four 3in/7cm brass hinges*
◆ *One large roll garden twine (or string of your choice)*
◆ *465 crystal oval glass beads (1 x ¾in/26 x 20mm)*
◆ *300 crystal disc glass beads (¾in/18mm)*
◆ *96 crystal disc glass beads (1 x ¼in/25 x 4mm)*
◆ *Approximately 2oz/56g candle wax*
◆ *Old tin and saucepan*
◆ *Newspaper*
◆ *Drill and wood drill bits*
◆ *Small round wood file*
◆ *Measuring tape*
◆ *Pencil*
◆ *Medium-grade sandpaper*
◆ *White latex/emulsion paint*
◆ *2in/4cm paintbrush and sponge*
◆ *All purpose clear adhesive*
◆ *Clear wood sealer*

1 Make up the screen with the wood and hinges. The screen has three panels: each has two lengths 63in/160cm tall and two 18in/46cm pieces across the width, one at top and one 3⅛in/8cm up from the bottom.

2 Work on one panel at a time. On the inside top and bottom of each frame, mark 14 points (or any even number of your choice) with a pencil at 1¼in/3cm apart.

3 Using a drill bit closest to the correct size for your gauge of twine, drill holes all the way from the inside out on the frame. Run the wood file into the holes to clear them. Use the sandpaper to clean the edges of the holes and all relevant surfaces.

4 To get a "whitewashed" effect on the frame, add 2 tablespoons of the white paint to 16fl oz/400ml of water and mix well.

5 Soak a sponge, wring it out to just damp and rub it all over the frame once, then go back layering the paint to reach the density that you prefer. If some areas get too dense, wipe them down with a clean wet sponge to remove some of the paint.

6 Leave to dry, then apply a thin coat of the clear wood sealer and leave to dry for 24 hours.

7 Measure the height of the frame from floor to top and multiply by three. Cut lengths of twine to this measurement for half the total number of holes across the top of the frame. (For 42 holes you need to cut 21 lengths.)

8 Put the candle wax into a tin can, and place inside a saucepan with enough water to cover the bottom. Gently heat the saucepan to melt the wax, then carefully remove the tin.

9 Dip the ends of the twine up to 5in/ 12cm to coat them, keeping the wax application thin. Lay them out straight on some old newspaper to harden. This will make it easier to pass the twine through the holes in the framework and the beads.

10 Take a length of twine and run it up through the first hole in the top of one of the panels of the frame and back down through the next hole, keeping the two hanging halves equal. Continue to thread the remaining holes in the panel.

11 Follow the chart in the back of the book for the beading sequence and measurements. Use one or two overhand knots under each bead to hold it in place.

12 Start beading across the rows from the top, then down row by row, measuring the distances between the beads to keep them even.

13 When you reach the bottom of each panel push the waxed ends of twine through the drilled holes in the bottom of the frame.

14 Leave for a couple of days to allow the twine to stretch with the weight of the beads: you may at that point need to readjust the beads at the bottom.

15 To finish off the screen, tie off the twine in pairs on the underside of the bottom of the frame, double knotting each pair. Don't pull the twine too taut but make sure that the knot is tight.

16 Apply a small amount of clear adhesive to each knot and leave to dry. Cut off the excess twine close to the knots.

▶ 87

stained glass vase

✚

Find scraps of colored and textured glass at a stained glass artist's workshop or artist's supply store.

MATERIALS

◆ *Large glass vase 15¾ x 6¾in/ 40 x 17cm*
◆ *Stained glass scraps in blues and greens*
◆ *Permanent marker*
◆ *Glass cutter*
◆ *Protective goggles*
◆ *Contact adhesive*
◆ *Small narrow paintbrush*
◆ *Waterproof grout*
◆ *Spatula*
◆ *Squeegee*
◆ *Sponge*
◆ *Steel wool scourer*
◆ *Clear floor wax*

1 Enlarge the template on a photocopier to fit around the inside of the vase.

2 With the lines facing out, draw over the pattern on the outside of the glass with a permanent marker. Remove the paper template from the vase.

3 Choose one shade of glass for the main lines in the drawing. Score the pieces into strips (approximately ¼in/17mm wide) and tap along the back of each score line with the ball end of the glass cutter.

4 Score the strips into small rectangles, ½–⅞in/1–2cm long and tap these off.

5 With the paintbrush, paint contact adhesive over the main lines on the vase and leave to set. Working with a number of pieces at a time, paint one side of each piece of cut glass with a thin coat of contact adhesive and leave to set.

6 Press the glass in place over the lines, following the pattern and keeping the pieces close together.

7 Continue working the pattern outwards: surround each mosaic line with a different color of glass, and then work a "background" of patches of different shades of blues and greens to fill in all the spaces. Leave to set for 24 hours.

8 Spread grout over the surface of the tiles with a spatula, filling in all of the gaps. Using the squeegee, scrape off as much grout as you can.

9 Working next to running water, soak and wring out a sponge, and wipe down the vase, removing as much grout as you can. It won't all come off at this stage. Smooth out the top and bottom edges of the vase with some grout and a damp sponge. Leave to set for 12–24 hours.

10 With the scourer, gently rub the mosaic to remove any residual grout. Use a damp sponge to remove any grout dust. Rub on a light coat of the wax and leave to dry.

pebble chalkboard

✚

Spread the collections from your nature walks across the table and choose some striking textures, shapes, and colors.

MATERIALS
- *Framed chalkboard 15½ x 23in/ 38.5 x 58.5cm*
- *Saw*
- *Gray satin enamel paint*
- *Paintbrush*
- *Chalk*
- *Colored ultramarine-blue grout*
- *Rubber spatula*
- *Beach pebbles*
- *Wood glue*
- *¼ round wood molding/edging 31½in/80cm long*

1 Measure the inside of the frame from top to bottom and cut two pieces of ¼ round wood molding/edging with the saw to fit.

2 Paint these strips and the frame of the chalkboard with gray satin enamel paint. Leave to dry.

3 From the inside edge of each side of the frame measure a panel on the chalkboard 4½in/11.5cm wide. Draw a line from top to bottom. Spread these panels with colored grout, keeping the inside edge clean and smoothing over the top with a rubber spatula.

4 While the grout is still wet, paint the back of each strip of wood molding/edging with wood glue and stick them into place alongside the edge of the colored grout.

5 Top up the side panels with more colored grout, smoothing the top over with a wet rubber spatula, and taking care not to get it on the edges of the frame. Stick pebbles in an interesting pattern into the grout while still wet. Leave to dry in a cool place for 24 hours.

round platter

✚

Always take care when smashing the white tiles. Do it outside and wear goggles to protect your eyes.

MATERIALS

- ◆ *Round wooden plate 40in/102cm in circumference, 12½in/32cm in diameter*
- ◆ *Four 6in/15cm square white tiles*
- ◆ *Four 4in/10cm square sheets of ¾in/2cm square red glass mosaic tiles*
- ◆ *Course sandpaper*
- ◆ *Pair of compasses and pencil*
- ◆ *Sack or strong garbage bag*
- ◆ *Hammer*
- ◆ *Protective goggles*
- ◆ *Tile nippers*
- ◆ *Waterproof grout/adhesive*
- ◆ *Artist's palette knife*
- ◆ *Grout spreader*
- ◆ *Sponge*
- ◆ *Matte white latex/emulsion paint*
- ◆ *Paintbrush*
- ◆ *Soft cloth*
- ◆ *Clear floor wax*

1 Sand the front and back surfaces of the plate to remove any varnish and "key" the surface for grouting.

2 Measure and mark the center of the plate and with the compasses draw six consecutive circles, approximately 1in/2.5cm apart. This will give you seven rings, counting the center dot.

3 Soak the red mosaic tiles in water for 15 minutes and remove the backing paper. Leave to dry. Put the white tiles in a sack and smash with a hammer to get a variety of shapes and sizes. Using tile nippers cut most of the red tiles into quarters.

4 Use the nippers to round off the edges of one whole red tile to go in the center of the plate. "Butter" the back of the tile with a little waterproof grout applied with an artist's palette knife, and stick in place.

5 To make the next circle, apply grout to some of the white tile shards with the palette knife and press firmly in place. Work in sections around the ring, using the nippers to "reshape" tiles as needed to fit the shape.

6 For the next circle, grout some red tile quarters and apply them, working around the circle. Continue working out to the edge of the plate, alternating the colors. Leave to set for 24 hours.

7 Spread grout over the entire surface with the grout spreader, filling in all gaps and crevices. Scrape the surface clear of all excess grout and wipe with a damp sponge until the tiled surface is clean. Wipe a smooth edge of grout around the outside edge, smoothing with a clean damp sponge. Leave to set for 24 hours.

8 Turn the plate over and paint the bottom and any exposed edges with matte white latex/emulsion paint. Leave to dry.

9 Wipe the tiled surface with a soft cloth and apply a thin coat of the floor wax. Leave to dry. Always handwash.

house numbers

✚

If you can't get copper foil in strips, take a sheet of ¹⁄₁₆in/1mm copper foil, mark it up into ¾in/2cm strips and cut out.

MATERIALS

◆ ½in/12mm treated/external medium density fiberboard (MDF) or plywood
◆ 1mm thickness soft copper foil in ¾in/2cm strips
◆ Broken glass in various colors and sizes
◆ 5lb/2.5kg white cement
◆ 2lb/1kg silver sand
◆ Drill and ¹⁄₁₆in bit
◆ Jigsaw and medium-grade blade
◆ Workbench
◆ Medium-grade sandpaper
◆ Contact cement
◆ Hammer
◆ ½in/8mm copper hardboard pins/nails
◆ PVA glue
◆ Picture hanging wire
◆ Pencil and knife

1 Enlarge the relevant templates on a photocopier (my numbers were 24 x 18in/60 x 45cm. Cut out and trace onto the MDF.

2 Cut out each number with a jigsaw using a medium blade. Sand all edges.

3 Hold each number between thumb and forefinger close to the top edge to find the point where it hangs straight. Mark this point and drill two holes one inch apart. Sand the holes and run a 5in/12cm piece of picture wire through the holes. Knot at the back.

4 Wrap the copper foil around the numbers overlapping the strips slightly. Remove the foil and paint the edges of the numbers and the edge of the copper foil where it will meet the wood with contact cement. Leave to set, then press the foil firmly into place. Nail copper nails around the edging 7cm/3in apart.

5 Paint a thin coat of glue over the surface of the number and into the gaps between the wood and copper. Leave to dry.

6 To mix up the white cement, measure out 2 portions cement to 1 portion silver sand. Make enough to do one number at a time. Stir the water in slowly until the cement won't hold any more when you stop stirring. Pour off any water sitting on top. Leave to stand for two to three minutes, then pour into the number form, spreading it with a knife if necessary.

7 Immediately begin pressing in bits of glass until you've filled in as many gaps as possible, spreading the colors and sizes evenly throughout. Leave to set.

window box

✚

Using frostproof grout and adhesive will protect the mosaic surface of the window box against the elements.

MATERIALS
◆ Clay window box 6 x 16½in/ 15 x 42cm
◆ Frostproof adhesive
◆ Artist's palette knife
◆ Grout spreader
◆ Four 4in/10cm square tiles in each color of lime and grass green
◆ Ten 4in/10cm square light dusky pink clay tiles
◆ Two 4in/10cm square dark dusky pink tiles
◆ Frostproof grout
◆ PVA glue
◆ Thin card
◆ Scissors
◆ Permanent marker
◆ Newspaper
◆ Protective goggles
◆ Tile nippers
◆ Sponge
◆ Soft cloth
◆ Clear floor wax

92 ◀

1 Mix frostproof adhesive with water to a spreadable consistency. With a palette knife and grout spreader cover the outside of the window box with a thin even coat of frostproof adhesive. This will keep any lime from seeping out through the clay and give you a flat even surface to work on. Leave to set for 12 hours.

2 Photocopy the leaf templates, adjusting the size to fit the height dimension of your window box if necessary. Glue the photocopies to thin card and cut out. Hold the templates in position on the sides of the window box and draw around them with a permanent marker.

3 Remove all the tiles from their backing paper by soaking them in water first; after 15 minutes the paper will slip off easily. Spread the tiles on newspaper to dry.

4 Cut two thirds of the two green colored tiles into quarters with tile nippers. The rest you may need for cutting odd shapes; cut as you need them.

5 Begin to mosaic the central leaf design from the inside line to one outside edge in one shade of green and then the other half in the other shade of green. Trim and shape the tiles as you need to. "Butter" the backs with a small amount of the tile adhesive on the end of an artist's palette knife and stick them firmly in position.

6 Complete all the leaf shapes and leave to dry for 24 hours.

7 For the background, cut most of the light pink tiles into quarters with the tile nippers. Stick the tile pieces as before around the leaf patterns creating even horizontal rows as you go. Nip and cut the pieces as needed. Work all the way around the window box leaving the top rim free of pattern. Leave to set for 12–24 hours.

8 Cut the rest of the light pink tiles into quarters and each of the dark pink tiles into three strips. Apply in a horizontal striped pattern around the entire rim of the window box, nipping and trimming tiles as you need. Leave to set for 24 hours.

9 Mix the frostproof grout to a thick, creamy consistency and apply to the entire tiled surface of the box, scraping it across the surface to fill all cracks and gaps and blending around the edges. Scrape off the excess grout and wipe the surface with a clean damp sponge. Keep wiping until the tiles come clean.

10 Smooth some grout over the top rim of the window box to avoid the contrast of the terra-cotta clay. Smooth this edge over with a clean damp sponge. Leave to dry for 24 hours.

11 Wipe the tiled surface of the window box with a soft cloth and then apply a thin coat of clear floor wax. Leave to dry.

Detail showing the central fig leaf design.

mirror frame

✚

Ask a local mirror and glass store to cut a piece of mirror to fit the size of the window in your frame. The one used here measures 4in/10cm square. Alternatively, use the frame to display a decorative postcard, picture, or favorite photograph.

MATERIALS

◆ *Wooden picture frame with a wide edge. (This one measures 2³⁄₄in/7cm.)*
◆ *Four ³⁄₈in/1cm square mirror tiles*
◆ *Six small triangular mirror tiles*
◆ *Six ³⁄₄in/2cm square red glass mosaic tiles*
◆ *Six ³⁄₄in/2cm square bright blue glass mosaic tiles*
◆ *Artist's charcoal or chalk*
◆ *Masking tape*
◆ *Soft lead pencil or permanent marker*
◆ *White packaging/parcel string*
◆ *Scissors*
◆ *PVA glue*
◆ *Rubber gloves*
◆ *Polyfilla*
◆ *Plaster of Paris*
◆ *Plastic bowls or containers*
◆ *Newspaper*
◆ *Fine-grade sandpaper*
◆ *Semi-gloss white latex/emulsion paint*
◆ *³⁄₄in/2cm soft bristled paintbrush*
◆ *Clear floor wax*
◆ *Protective goggles*
◆ *Tile nippers*
◆ *Tile adhesive*
◆ *Artist's palette knife*

Finished size: 9¹⁄₂in/24cm square

1 Enlarge the template to fit the frame. Remove any glass and backing boards from the frame.

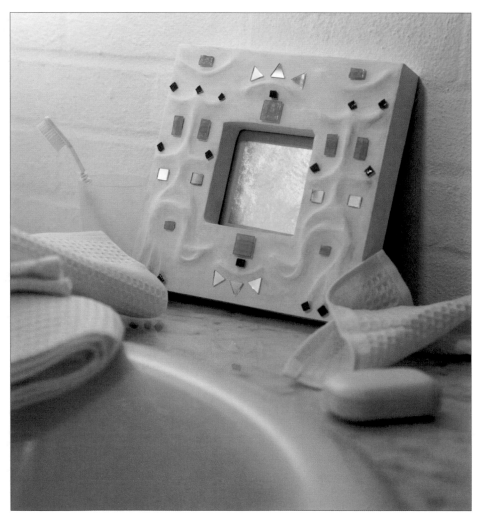

94 ◀

2 Rub the back of the photocopy with artist's charcoal and tape in place on top of the frame.

3 Draw over the lines with a sharpened soft lead pencil to transfer them to the frame. You do not need to draw over the lines that show the positions of the pieces of glass and mirror.

4 Remove the tape and the template and draw over the images with the pencil or permanent marker.

5 Cut workable lengths of string and place in a container with PVA glue. Leave to soak for five minutes.

6 Remove and stick in place over the lines on the frame, trimming to the correct length. Leave to dry.

7 Start building up the form around the string "drawings" by applying polyfilla to mound up the shapes into little hills. Fill in any gaps that appear between the string and the wood, and wet your finger to smooth over the surface. Leave to dry (*see picture next column*).

8 Use plaster of Paris in small quantities, mixing it up as you need it, as it sets very quickly. To get the correct consistency, pour a small amount of powder into a bowl or container and pour in water, stirring continually. When the plaster will not hold any more water, it is ready. (It should be the consistency of heavy cream.)

9 Smooth the plaster all over the surface of the frame with your fingers (you could wear rubber gloves for this). Leave to set.

10 Build up the surface in layers until the frame is completely covered; about three applications should be enough. On the final layer before the plaster sets, smooth the surface over with water on your fingers. Leave to dry overnight.

11 Lightly sand the plastered surface to smooth any ridges and remove any dribbles on the sides of the frame.

12 Paint the side edges of the frame inside and out with two coats of semi-gloss white latex/emulsion paint. Leave to dry.

13 With a soft bristled brush paint a thin layer of clear floor wax over the surface of plaster. Leave to dry.

14 Cut the blue and red glass tiles into halves and then again into thirds using the tile nippers

15 Apply the cut glass and mirror tiles where indicated on the template by "buttering" a small amount of tile adhesive to the back of each tile using an artist's palette knife and pressing firmly into position. Use the tile nippers to nip any pieces into shape, using the color code on the template as a guide. Leave to dry.

16 Place the mirror/glass inside the frame and reinsert the backing boards to finish.

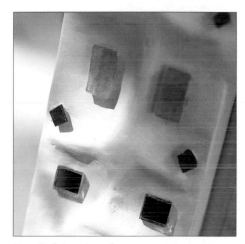

Detail of the mirror frame.

plant stand

✚

The pre-Columbians worshipped the sun. By recreating their traditional patterns for this plant stand you could create a small haven of sun worship for your favorite plant in the house.

MATERIALS

◆ *Wooden plant stand on metal base with 46¹⁄₂in/118cm circumference, 14in/35.5cm diameter, 1in/2.5cm thickness*
◆ *One sheet (size 13¹⁄₂in/36cm square) each of 1in/2.5cm square floor tiles in cobalt blue, medium blue, ice blue, and coral pink*
◆ *Waterproof grout/adhesive*
◆ *Tracing paper*
◆ *PVA glue*
◆ *2in/5cm paintbrush*
◆ *Adhesive tape*
◆ *Charcoal*
◆ *Sharp pencil*
◆ *Protective goggles*
◆ *Tile nippers*
◆ *Artist's palette knife*
◆ *Grout spreader*
◆ *Sponge*
◆ *Soft cloth*
◆ *Clear floor wax*
◆ *Sandpaper*

1 If possible remove the top from the stand. Sand the edges and top to "key" the surface. Mix 2 parts PVA glue to 1 part water and brush a thin layer over the top and sides. Leave to dry.

2 Photocopy the template. To enlarge this copy on a normal photocopier draw lines

across the pattern to quarter the page, and enlarge each quarter page to get the correct size when pieced together. Tape all four copies together, carefully joining up the zigzag pattern.

3 Trace the pattern onto tracing paper and rub the back with charcoal. Place in position on the table top and draw over the pattern with a sharpened pencil. Remove the tracing paper and draw over the pattern on the table top with the pencil.

4 Remove the backing paper from all the tiles. If the backing is mesh, just pull the tiles off: if the backing is paper, soak the tiles first for 15 minutes in water, then peel away the paper. Leave to dry.

5 Begin the mosaic pattern by first working the coral pink tiles. With the tile nippers, cut a quantity of tiles in half and lay them out in position on the table top. Use the nippers to shape the tiles for the bends in the pattern and around the edges of the table.

6 Stick the tiles down by "buttering" the backs of the tiles with grout/adhesive spread on thinly with an artist's palette knife. Stick the tiles securely in position;

keep all edges of tiles and the exposed surface of the table top clean of grout/adhesive as this will hinder the placement of the blue tiles. Leave to dry for 24 hours.

7 Stick the three shades of blue tiles in the same way, using the main picture as a reference. Leave to dry for 24 hours.

8 To mosaic the edge of the table, simply continue the color patterns on the top of the table and stick on tile halves all around the edge. Leave to dry for 24 hours.

9 Spread waterproof grout over the table top with a grout spreader to cover the

entire surface and edges. To facilitate working on the edges, raise the tabletop onto something to lift it off your work surface. (I used an upside down pie dish.)

10 Scrape all excess grout off the surface and smooth around the edging tiles top and bottom. Wipe with a clean damp sponge until the tile surfaces are clean, rinsing the sponge as you work. Smooth over more grout around the table to give a finished edge and wipe smooth with a wet sponge. Leave to dry for 24 hours.

11 Wipe the table top with a clean soft cloth and apply a thin coat of clear floor wax to the tiles to finish the surface. Reattach the top to the stand.

Detail showing the edge of the plant stand.

bathroom back splash

✚

As each of these trout takes on its own personality you'll find yourself charmed into the rhythm of mosaicking.

MATERIALS
◆ ¾in/2cm thick sheet of plywood, cut to 16 x 19in/41 x 48cm
◆ 4in/10cm square sheet of ¾in/2cm ceramic mosaic tiles in the following quantities: four salmon pink; nine speckled gray; three dark gray; one green/gray; four dark blue/green; four pale blue; four blue/gray; two dark blue
◆ Drill and bits
◆ Medium-grade sandpaper
◆ PVA glue
◆ Pencil
◆ Thin card
◆ Protective goggles
◆ Tile nippers
◆ Waterproof grout/adhesive
◆ Artist's palette knife
◆ Sponge
◆ Grout spreader
◆ Screws and wall sinkers
◆ Screwdriver
◆ Soft cloth
◆ Clear floor wax

1 If the back splash is to be secured to a wall, first measure and mark four corners for screw holes in the plywood. Drill these out with a drill bit the correct size for the screws to be used.

2 Sand the surface and edges of the plywood. Mix 2 parts PVA glue to 1 part water and brush this on the front and edges. Leave to dry.

3 Photocopy the fish and border pattern templates, stick these onto thin card and cut out.

4 Place in position on the plywood with even spacing between and trace around them with a pencil.

5 Soak all the tiles in water for 15 mintues and peel away their paper backing. Lay them out to dry.

6 Begin tiling the fish by working each one from the inside out, starting with the pink

line in the center of each. Cut a small quantity of pink tiles into quarters with a pair of tile nippers. Nip each quarter to fit the shape of the pattern. Place them in position, working through all of the pink lines before sticking.

7 "Butter" a small amount of grout onto the backs of the cut tiles with an artist's palette knife and stick them down securely.

8 Do the same with the speckled gray and dark gray to complete the body and add the eye from the green/gray tile.

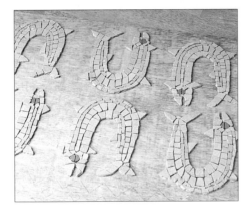

9 Complete all the fish and leave to dry as you work on the border.

10 Cut the gray and green/gray tiles for the border into quarters and lay them all out in the pattern before sticking them down. Use the main picture as a reference. Avoid covering over the holes drilled in the corners. Leave to dry for 24 hours.

11 To lay the background, cut the four shades of blue tiles into quarters. Begin working the pattern from around the fish outward in a grid pattern. Fill in all of the background keeping a random color mix. Leave the drilled holes exposed but cut

four tiles for their places and keep to one side. When the background is complete, leave to dry for 24 hours.

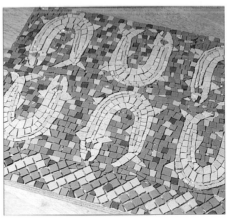

12 Spread the surface of the mosaic with a generous quantity of grout and fill in all holes and gaps (except for the drilled holes) with the grout spreader. With the spreader, scrape off as much excess grout as possible.

13 Using the grout spreader and a damp sponge spread grout around the edges of the plywood, and smooth the surface over with a damp sponge to hide the edges of the plywood.

14 With a clean damp sponge, wipe the mosaic surface clean, rinsing and wiping as much as is needed, to clear the surface of grout. Leave to dry for 24 hours.

15 Wipe the surface of the mosaic with a soft cloth to clear off any residue.

16 Mark and drill holes in the wall where the mosaic is to be placed, put in sinkers and screw the back splash into place.

17 Use a small amount of grout to fill in the gaps over the screw heads and stick the tiles for the four corner holes. Rub a small amount of grout across the surface to fill in any gaps, wipe clean and leave to dry.

18 To give a clear shine to the surface, wipe a thin film of clear floor wax over the surface and around the edges over the grout. Leave to dry.

Detail showing border and a fish's face.

birdhouse

✛

This tiled birdhouse is designed to sit on top of a tree stump or perch in the branches of a tree.

MATERIALS

- ◆ *½in/12mm treated/external large MDF or plywood scraps from a lumber store/ builder's merchant*
- ◆ *Five 4in/10cm square ceramic tiles in each color of dark blue, violet and orange*
- ◆ *Ten 6in/15cm square white ceramic wall tiles*
- ◆ *Three ¾in/2cm square gold glass mosaic tiles*
- ◆ *Two ¾in/2cm square light blue glass mosaic tiles*
- ◆ *Cardboard*
- ◆ *PVA glue*
- ◆ *Scissors or craft knife*
- ◆ *Jigsaw with medium blade*
- ◆ *Workbench*
- ◆ *Sandpaper*
- ◆ *Marker pen*
- ◆ *Wood glue*
- ◆ *1in/2.5cm wood nails/panel pins*
- ◆ *Hammer*
- ◆ *Protective goggles*
- ◆ *Tile cutter and nippers*
- ◆ *Notched grout spreader*
- ◆ *Waterproof tile adhesive*
- ◆ *Scouring pad*
- ◆ *Small round paintbrush*
- ◆ *Cleaning cloth*
- ◆ *Soft cloth*
- ◆ *Waterproof black grout*

1 Enlarge the template for the front of the birdhouse to measure 9in/23cm square to the top of the arch. Glue to the card-board and cut out. Sort out your scraps of MDF and find a piece large enough for the facade. Place the cardboard template on the MDF and draw around it.

2 On other scraps of the MDF, measure and mark two sides, a bottom, top, and back to the following sizes:
Sides: 6 x 5½in/15 x 14cm
Back: 8¾ x 5½in/22 x 14cm
Top: 8¾ x 6in/22 x 15.5cm
Bottom: 8¾ x 6½in/22 x 16cm

3 Using the jigsaw on a workbench, cut out all the pieces for the birdhouse. Sand all the edges.

4 With wood glue attach the front face on to the side panels setting the sides behind the edges of the front wall. Glue on the back. Leave to dry.

5 Secure the birdhouse structure by nail-ing the sides to the front and back with the nails/panel pins. Put three nails along each of the four sides – one at each end and one in the middle.

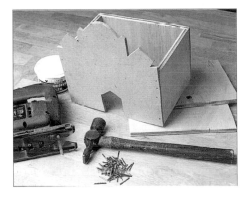

6 Attach the top and bottom to the sides with glue and nails/pins in the same way (*see picture next column*).

7 Begin tiling the birdhouse one surface at a time from the front facade. Cut tiles with a tile cutter and shape the edges with a tile nipper. Lay the tiles out on the drawing template until the design meshes together using gold tiles to highlight areas and small pieces of glass tile for details.

8 To apply the tiles, use the notched spreader with waterproof tile adhesive and work over the whole front facade trans-ferring cut tiles from the door surround outward. Press the tiles on firmly.

9 While you cut the tiles for the next sur-face the adhesive will have had time to set hard enough so that you can move the house around. Cover all the surfaces with various patterns of angular tiles. Keep the tile surfaces free of adhesive. Leave to set for 24 hours.

10 To apply the black grout, follow the manufacturer's instructions and apply to one surface at a time with a spreader and then wipe with a clean damp cloth. Leave to dry before going on to the next side. Cover and fill in all of the edges around the house, leave to dry, then fill in the edges on the top and bottom.

11 Mix up a small amount of black grout to a thick paint consistency and paint it around the inside of the door frame, on the floor at the entrance and onto the back of the top arch of the birdhouse facade, and all exposed edges. By this time the tiles will be fairly messy with grout on them.

12 Leave to dry for 24 hours and then go back over the tiles with a scouring pad to clean off any excess grout. Wipe clean with a dry soft cloth.

Detail of the birdhouse facade.

beaded screen

repeat the sequence as required

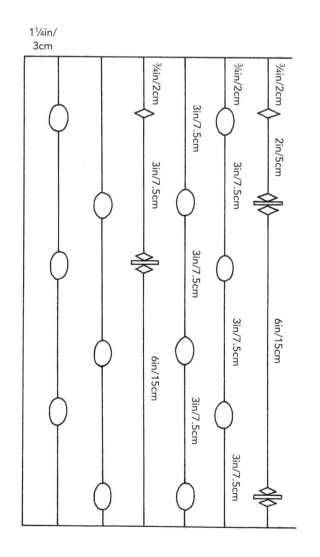

1¼in/
3cm

¾in/2cm

¾in/2cm

¾in/2cm

¾in/2cm

2in/5cm

3in/7.5cm

3in/7.5cm

3in/7.5cm

3in/7.5cm

3in/7.5cm

3in/7.5cm

3in/7.5cm

6in/15cm

6in/15cm

bead-embroidered cushion

enlarge template in two equal halves to reach an outer edge of 18in/45.5cm. Use the whole template twice to complete the square.

stained glass vase

enlarge as required

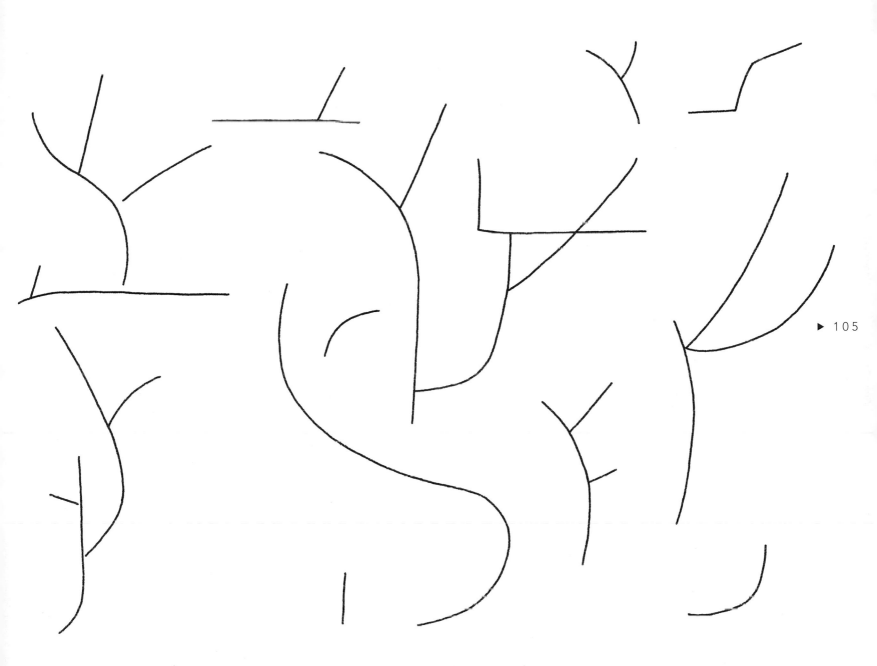

▶ 105

mirror frame

enlarge as required

Red   Blue   Mirror

window box
actual size

TEMPLATES

house numbers

enlarge as required

use a reverse no.6
for no.9

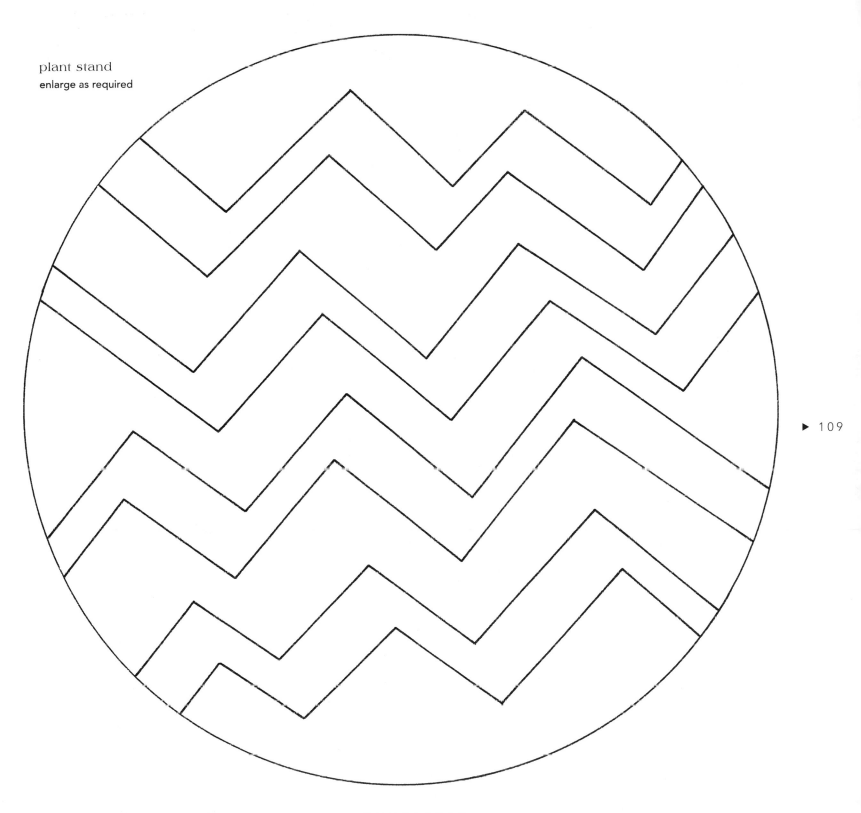

plant stand
enlarge as required

► 109

birdhouse

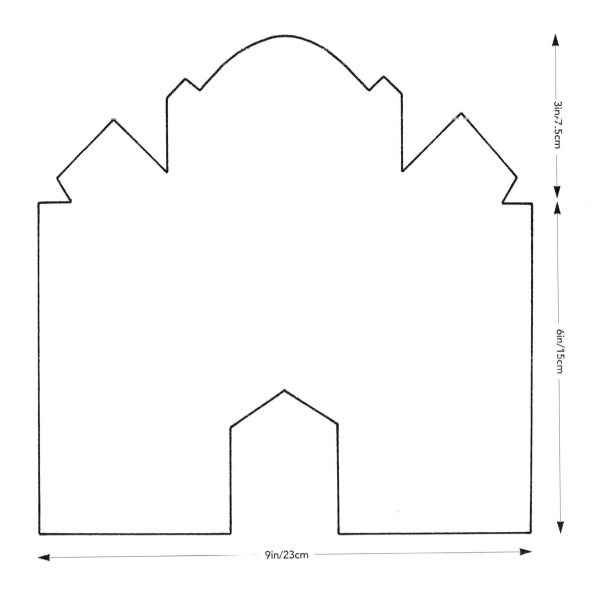

3in/7.5cm

6in/15cm

9in/23cm

► 111

index

✳